# Money

*This math series is dedicated to Nick, Tony, Riley, and Hailey.*

**Published by The Child's World®**
PO Box 326
Chanhassen, MN 55317-0326
800-599-READ
www.childsworld.com

Design and Production:
The Creative Spark, San Juan Capistrano, CA

Photos: © David M. Budd Photography

**Library of Congress Cataloging-in-Publication Data**
Pistoia, Sara.
 Money / by Sara Pistoia.
     p. cm. — (Mighty math series) (Easy reader)
Summary: Introduces the concept of money along with the values of
different coins.
 ISBN 1-56766-116-5 (lib. bdg. : alk. paper)
 1. Counting—Juvenile literature. 2. Coins, American—Juvenile
literature. [1. Money. 2. Coins. 3. Counting.] I. Title. II. Series.
III. Easy reader (Child's World (Firm))
 QA113 .P565 2002
 513.2—dc21
                                    2002002585

# Money

Sara Pistoia

# How do we use money?

We use money to buy things. We give someone money. They give us something in return. Using money is a form of trading.

Hi! I'm Math Mutt! I'll help you learn about money.

Long ago, people did not use money. When they needed something, they traded other items or their time.

Today people use money instead. They sell items or their time and get money in return. Then they use the money to buy things.

Money makes trading easier. Money comes as coins or paper bills. Each kind is worth a certain amount.

6

Counting is important when you use money.

penny = one cent     nickel = five cents

# Have you seen these coins?

dime = ten cents

quarter =
twenty-five cents

Can you count these pennies?
Each penny is worth one cent.
You need to count by ones.

Do you know the symbol for cents?
It's ¢. Twelve pennies equal 12¢!

10

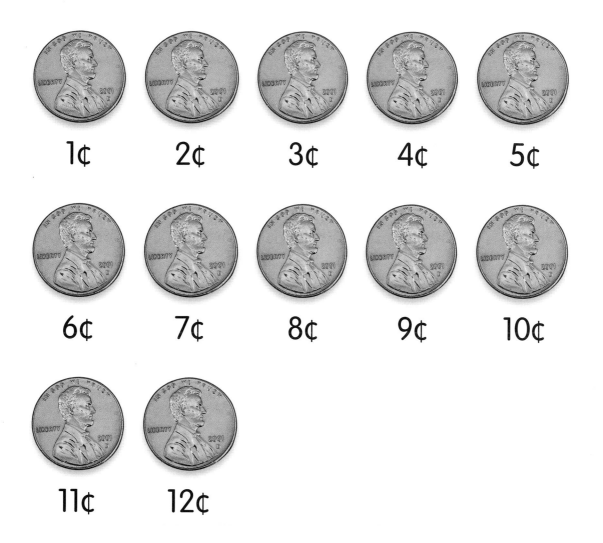

1¢    2¢    3¢    4¢    5¢

6¢    7¢    8¢    9¢    10¢

11¢    12¢

Did you count to twelve? That
means you have twelve cents.

A dime is worth ten cents.
With dimes, you need to count
by tens.

# Try counting these dimes.

| 10¢ | 20¢ | 30¢ | 40¢ |

| 50¢ | 60¢ | 70¢ | 80¢ |

Wow! I have eighty cents!

This candy costs ten cents.
Do you have enough money
to buy it?

What is the easiest way to add up different
kinds of coins? Try starting with the ones
that are worth the most.

5¢    6¢    7¢    8¢    9¢    10¢

How much are one nickel and
five pennies worth? Are they
the same as one dime?
Count to find out!

If you have one quarter, you have twenty-five cents. You could trade your quarter for other coins. What coins could you get?

How many pennies equal a quarter?

# Five nickels equal one quarter.

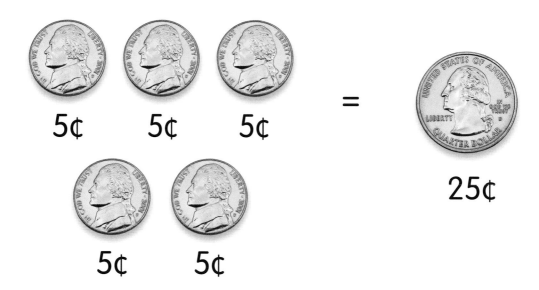

5¢    5¢    5¢    =

5¢    5¢

25¢

# Two dimes and one nickel equal a quarter. Count them and see!

10¢    10¢    +    5¢    =    25¢

Do you have enough money to buy this toy?

Start counting with the coin that is worth the most.

Finish with the coin that is worth the least.

25¢     35¢     40¢     45¢

46¢     47¢     48¢     49¢

You didn't have enough money?

What coin could you add so that you could buy this toy?

One more penny would be just enough.

Do you earn money for helping at home? Count the coins you have earned by doing chores.

25¢         35¢         45¢         50¢

I'm going to save all my money so I can buy something cool!

Money is part of our lives.

You can spend money and you can save money.

It's important to know how to count money!

# Key Words

buy

cent

dime

earn

equal

money

nickel

penny

quarter

trading

# Index

## About the Author

Sara Pistoia is a retired elementary teacher living in Southern California with her husband and a variety of pets. After 40 years of teaching, she now contributes to education by supervising and training student teachers at California State University at Fullerton. In authoring this series, she draws on the experience of many years of teaching first and second graders.